# Wedding Etiquette

Antonia Swinson

# Wedding

# Etiquette

RYLAND
PETERS
& SMALL
LONDON NEW YORK

*Designer* Sarah Walden
*Commissioning Editor* Annabel Morgan
*Picture Researcher* Emily Westlake
*Production* Patricia Harrington
*Art Director* Gabriella Le Grazie
*Publishing Director* Alison Starling

First published in the United States in
2003
by Ryland Peters & Small, Inc.
519 Broadway
Fifth Floor
New York, NY 10012
www.rylandpeters.com
Text, design, and photographs
© Ryland Peters & Small 2003
10 9 8 7 6 5 4 3 2

Printed and bound in China

ISBN 1 84172 512 9

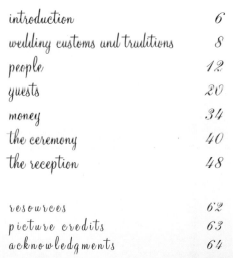

# contents

introduction     6

wedding customs and traditions     8

people     12

guests     20

money     34

the ceremony     40

the reception     48


resources     62

picture credits     63

acknowledgments     64

# introduction

How should you word your wedding invitations? Who sits at the top table? Can the bride make a toast at the reception? All these important questions and many, many more are answered in this beautiful and useful little guide to modern wedding etiquette.

*Each section takes a closer look at different elements of a wedding. **People** provides the lowdown on the roles and responsibilities of the members of the wedding party, and **Guests** tells you all you need to know on the subject of invitations and the bridal registry. **Money** covers the tricky subject of who pays for what. The practicalities of flowers, transportation, and the wedding processional are discussed in **The Ceremony**, while **The Reception** takes a look at the etiquette of the seating plan, the toasts, and the cutting of the cake.*

*This little book aims to be a friendly guide, leading you through the maze of wedding etiquette by providing advice on when it's best to stick to tradition...and when it's fine to break the rules!*

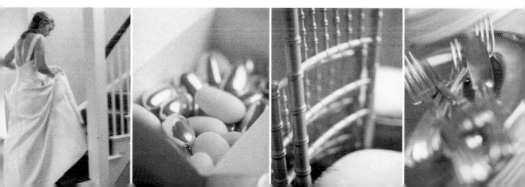

# wedding customs and traditions

♡ White weddings were a nineteenth-century invention. Before then, brides simply wore their best dress to get married in, sometimes with a white ribbon attached to symbolize purity.

♥ Veils were thought to keep away evil spirits, who would be confused by not being able to see the bride.

♡ In England, it's thought to be good luck to meet and kiss a chimney sweep on the way to the ceremony.

♥ The wedding ring symbolizes everlasting love. It's thought that the ancient Egyptians started the practice of wearing one on the third finger of the left hand—they believed that the vein in that finger ran straight to the heart.

♡ Throwing confetti has its roots in the Roman period, when guests threw almonds at newlyweds to symbolize a fruitful marriage.

♥ Cutting a cake at a wedding was once thought to ensure a fruitful marriage. Keeping a piece of cake is supposed to guarantee that your husband stays faithful.

♡ The honeymoon gets its name from the tradition of newlyweds drinking honeyed mead (a symbol of life and fertility) until the waning of the moon.

♥ Wedding receptions have their roots in the medieval period, when the groom had to demonstrate that he could support his wife by giving gifts of food and drink to his in-laws.

♡ Bouquets were originally posies of herbs, carried to ward off evil spirits.

Something old
something new
something borrowed
something blue
and a silver sixpence in your shoe

This verse refers to the bride's passage from her old life to her new one. "Something borrowed" means that marriage involves sharing; "something blue" alludes to the color's association with constancy; "and a silver sixpence in your shoe" refers to the hope of prosperity in marriage.

# People

*On the big day, the bride and groom are undoubtedly the stars of the show, but the best man, attendants, and groomsmen play very important supporting roles.*

# attendants and helpers

*The helpers* There are no hard and fast rules about attendants—whether or not you have bridesmaids and groomsmen is purely a matter of personal choice. If you're being married by a Justice of the Peace, you may not need groomsmen for the ceremony. It's usual to have a best man—some people even have two—and the best man could even be a best woman. There's a lot to think about when you're organizing a wedding, so if you do have attendants, make use of your maid of honor and best man when you need extra help before the day.

*Attendants* The bride may want to have a maid of honor (she's called this if she's single, and matron of honor if she's married). The maid of honor is the bride's right-hand woman on the day, so she should be well-organized and practical. If there isn't a maid of honor, distribute her duties (see next page) among your adult bridesmaids. There's no doubt that young flower girls and ring bearers add great charm to a wedding, but it can be a long and tiring day for them. The best man is the groom's chief helper and has a fairly long list of duties and a speech to make. He also needs to be organized and calm.

# *female members of the bridal party*

## *Maid of honor*

Her duties are:

- ♥ To organize the bachelorette party or bridal shower.
- ♡ To help the bride get ready before the wedding.
- ♥ To make sure that the bride's honeymoon luggage is sent to the reception venue or on to the hotel.
- ♡ To wait for the bride to arrive outside the ceremony venue and keep an eye on any young attendants.
- ♥ To arrange the bride's veil and train before she walks down the aisle.
- ♡ To take the bride's bouquet at the top of the aisle and look after it during the ceremony. She returns the bouquet to the bride for her walk back down the aisle.
- ♥ To look after the bride's dress once she's changed into her going-away outfit.

**The bride's mother** Traditionally, the bride's mother organizes the reception. Her duties include compiling the guest list, sending out invitations, organizing the flowers, ordering or making the cake, booking the photographer, and arranging accommodation for the guests. Nowadays, the bride or bridal couple assume many of these duties themselves. On the big day, the bride's mother usually helps dress the bride, supervises young flower girls, is present at the signing of the register, and may participate in the processional and recessional.

# male members of the bridal party

*The best man* is the groom's chief helper. His duties are:

♡ To arrange the bachelor party.

♥ To help organize outfits for himself, the groom, and the groomsmen, and to make sure they're collected.

♡ To help the groom get ready and get him to the ceremony.

♥ To coordinate and direct the groomsmen.

♡ To check that the boutonnieres arrive and that the program sheets are ready to be handed out.

♥ To look after the ring(s) and hand them to the officiant or groom during the ceremony.

♡ To make sure that any fees payable on the day are settled.

♥ To announce the toasts and the cake-cutting.

♡ To read out cards or messages at the reception and make the final toast.

♥ To announce the bride and groom's departure from the reception.

*Groomsmen* help everything run smoothly on the wedding day. The groomsmens' duties are:

♡ To hand out program sheets as guests arrive and to show them to their seats.

♥ To escort the bride's mother and groom's parents to their seats at the front of the church.

♡ To seat any latecomers.

♥ To get guests together for formal photographs.

# Guests

*Sharing your day with friends and family, whether it's a select few or a small army of them, will heighten the joy of your celebrations.*

# the guest list

♥ The size of your guest list is dictated by your budget. If you've set your heart on a certain location, this may also limit numbers. Once you've set a maximum head count, don't be tempted to exceed it. Don't rely on a dropout rate, either, because you'll be in trouble if all your guests accept.

♡ The easiest way to draw up a list is to start by including everyone you'd like to invite, then start eliminating names. This is a difficult process, but start by dropping people you haven't seen for several years. You're not obliged to invite colleagues from work or an escort for single friends. Most couples draw up their guest list with their parents. Even if the couple themselves, or the bride's parents, are footing the whole bill, it's only fair that everyone has a chance to say whom they'd like to invite.

♥ Deciding how to share out the list between the different parties demands diplomacy. Things can be difficult if parents feel their share of the guest list should be larger than the bride and groom would like. There may be distant relatives they want to invite for etiquette's sake, while you would rather invite more friends. Some couples have a two-tiered reception, inviting a small group of guests to the ceremony and meal, then having an evening party to which additional guests are invited.

♡ Remember that if you invite someone to your wedding, it should be because you really want them to be there, so you and your fiancé should have the final say.

## inviting children—yes or no

♥ Whether or not to invite children is a tricky decision. There are no rules of etiquette about whether or not to invite them—it depends on your own preference. Some people feel a wedding would not be complete without kids around, while others see it as an adult occasion.

♡ If you decide not to include children, it's diplomatic to let people know verbally, so that you can explain your reasons and avoid causing offence. Bear in mind that some guests won't be able to find babysitters for their children during your wedding and therefore won't be able to come.

♥ Whatever you decide, one decision must go for all. The only exception to this is your immediate family—it's natural to invite little nieces and nephews even if you're not having any other children.

♡ If you do include children, think about ways to keep them happy. If there are lots of them, hire an entertainer or provide an outdoor activity. Have a special children's table at the reception, complete with crayons and paper or toys and child-friendly food. There are also companies that provide babysitting services at weddings.

Mr and Mrs Christopher
request the pleasure of
your company at the marr...
of their daughter
Jennifer
to
Mr Robin Bi...
at the Church of St Pra...
on Saturday 1st Ma...
at 3 o'clock
and afterwards at
14 Birdcage Walk, sw...
... Road
... SW10 0RJ

# invitations

♥ Traditional invitations are printed in black on white or cream card, and may be hand-engraved (the most expensive option), thermographed (looks like hand engraving, but cheaper) or flat printed (the cheapest method). Traditional wordings are given on pages 28–29, but there's no reason why you shouldn't have something less formal if it suits the mood of your wedding.

♡ With formal invitations, guests' names are handwritten in the top left corner or in the space provided within the wording of the invitation, and full titles are used. If you're sending an invitation to a married couple, the correct form of address on the envelope is "Mr. and Mrs. Joseph Bloggs".

♥ It's good etiquette to send an invitation to the groom's parents and, if you're having a church wedding, to the minister.

♡ If your reception includes a formal dinner and dance, and you want guests to wear black tie and evening dress, "Black Tie" should be printed in the bottom right corner of your invitations.

♥ If you're having an evening party to which you're inviting extra guests, there should be a separate invitation for this.

♡ Send invitations out two or three months before the day to be safe, and certainly no later than six weeks before.

# wordings for invitations

Here are some standard and alternative wordings for wedding invitations. If you're hosting your own wedding, begin "Lauren Porter and Peter Kennedy request the pleasure of your company at their marriage..."

invitation to a wedding, bride's parents as hosts:

*Mr. and Mrs. Jeff Gleason*
*request the honour of your presence*
*at the marriage of their daughter*
*Lauren Ann*
*to*
*Mr. Peter Kennedy*
*at Saint Michael's Church, Wilbury,*
*on Saturday, the Twenty-Sixth of July*
*Two Thousand and Three*
*at 3 o'clock*
*and afterwards at*
*The Hampton Hotel, Wilbury*

invitation to a wedding, bride's parents as hosts (alternative wording):

*Mr. and Mrs. Jeff Gleason*
*request the honour of the presence of*
*[name of guest(s) written by hand]*
*at the marriage of their daughter*
*Lauren Ann*
*to*
*Mr. Peter Kennedy*
*at Saint Michael's Church, Wilbury,*
*on Saturday, the Twenty-Sixth of July*
*Two Thousand and Three*
*at 3 o'clock*
*and afterwards at*
*The Hampton Hotel, Wilbury*

invitation to a wedding, bride's parents divorced and mother remarried:

*Mr. Jeff Gleason and Mrs. Anthony Ricci*
*request the honour of your presence*

If mother is not remarried, begin:

*Mr. Jeff Gleason and Mrs. Barbara Gleason*

invitation to a service of blessing:

*Mr. and Mrs. Jeff Gleason*
*request the honour of your presence*
*at the blessing of the marriage*
*of their daughter*
*Lauren Ann...*

*28 guests*

invitation to a wedding reception only:

Mr. and Mrs. Jeff Gleason
request the pleasure of your company
at a reception
following the marriage of their daughter
Lauren Ann...

invitation to an evening party only:

Mr. and Mrs. Jeff Gleason
request the pleasure of your company
at an evening party
following the marriage of their daughter
Lauren Ann...

---

invitation to a wedding at home or a hotel:

Mr. and Mrs. Jeff Gleason
request the pleasure of your company
at the marriage of their daughter
Lauren Ann
to
Mr Peter Kennedy
at The Hampton Hotel, Wilbury
on Saturday, the Twenty-Sixth of July
Two Thousand and Three
at 3 o'clock
and afterward at a reception

## other items of wedding stationery

**Place cards** If you're having a seating plan at your reception, you'll need place cards for the tables. These can be printed or handwritten.

**Reply cards** You don't have to include pre-printed reply cards and addressed envelopes with your invitations, though they may encourage guests to reply promptly.

*Rachel*

*Menus* These are optional. Your hotel or caterer may be able to supply them, so ask before you order printed ones.

*Table plans* You'll need one of these if you're having a seated meal, well displayed so guests can easily see where to sit.

*Table stationery* You may want to go the whole hog and order coasters, napkins, matchbooks, and so on with your names or initials and the date of your wedding.

*Thankyous* You must take the trouble of handwriting a personal thankyou for any gifts. Tackle them as presents arrive.

*Program sheets* These contain details of the order of service, music, and readings, to make it easy for everyone to follow.

# the gift registry

♥ A gift registry serves a practical purpose, saving you from ten-toasters syndrome. It also makes life easy for your guests, who can be confident they've bought you something you really want.

♡ On the other hand, it's important that you don't appear to be greedy or asking for gifts. Although many stores provide cards detailing where the list is held and these cards can be enclosed with the wedding invitations, it is not considered good etiquette to do so. However, many people do so nowadays.

♥ More and more companies are offering a gift registry service, from department stores to specialty stores (and there's nothing to stop you registering at more than one place). There are also registry companies that deal with many different suppliers, giving you an enormous choice of products and brands.

♡ A gift registry used to help couples to set up home and consisted of household basics—bed linen, china, glassware, and so on. However, if you live together already or have been married before, these basics are probably redundant. You may, therefore, want decorative items for your home or garden, or something special, such as wine or books. If you want to put expensive items on your list, some stores allow guests to buy part of a gift. You may also be able to put gift vouchers on your list. However, it's not good etiquette to ask for money.

### *Gift registry do's and don'ts*

♥ Register well before your wedding so that your list is complete by the time your invitations are sent out.

♡ Going round a store making endless decisions can be exhausting, so split it up into a couple of trips if possible.

♥ Make sure your list covers a broad price range.

♡ Don't make your list too long or you'll end up with incomplete sets.

♥ Check the availability of items—there's nothing worse than finding that your china is about to be discontinued.

♡ Write your thankyous as gifts arrive, to save you a mountain of letters after your honeymoon. Letters should be personal and handwritten.

♥ Some guests will bring gifts on the day. Ask one of the bridesmaids or groomsmen to make sure they're safe and that cards are firmly stuck on gifts (give them a roll of tape). Someone (perhaps the bride's parents) will have to take home the gifts at the end of the reception.

# *Money*

*Traditionally, the bride's parents organized and paid for everything to do with the wedding. Nowadays, it's more common for both sets of parents to contribute or even for couples to pay for everything themselves.*

# the budget

♥ Work out who will pay for what and make sure that everyone is clear about what has been decided. Bear in mind that if someone is paying for something, they may feel that it gives them a say in how the money is spent. Be realistic about money: a wedding that's going to leave you financially strapped isn't a good start to married life.

♡ Most couples allocate their biggest chunk of money— around 50 per cent—to the reception. The other main areas, namely wedding clothes and accessories, music, photography, flowers, and other miscellaneous items (invitations, favors, and so on), will probably account for about 10 per cent each.

♥ Once you've set a budget, stick to it. Add a safety net for unforeseen costs. Get a couple of quotes for every service and remember that, to get an accurate figure, you must provide as much information as possible, especially the number of guests. Read all quotes carefully, including the small print. Watch out for hidden extras such as delivery costs or charges for extra staff. Make sure that all subsequent dealings with your suppliers are in writing and check when they need to know final numbers. File all your quotes and bills as they come in. Keep a running total so you know how on or off target you are.

♡ You'll almost certainly have to pay a deposit when you accept a quote. The balance will be due around the time of the wedding. Check whether you need to arrange for payments to be made while you are away on honeymoon.

# who pays for what

Below is the traditional breakdown of who pays for what.
However, these days, the bridal couple and both sets of parents
often share the wedding costs.

## The bride's parents

♡ Wedding stationery.

♥ The bride's outfit and accessories.

♡ The flowers for the ceremony and reception.

♥ The music for the ceremony and reception.

♡ The photographer and videographer.

♥ The transportation.

♡ The reception, including food and drink.

♥ The cake.

## The groom

♡ The bride's engagement and wedding rings.

♥ Bouquets for the bride and her attendants, corsages, and
boutonnieres.

♡ All ceremony or church fees (including organist and choir).

♥ Presents for the attendants, best man, and groomsmen.

♡ The first-night hotel.

♥ The honeymoon.

## The bride

♡ The groom's wedding ring.

# The Ceremony

Whether you exchange your vows
in a church, synagogue, or another
location, the marriage ceremony is
at the heart of the day. Then the
celebrations can begin.

# flowers

*The bride's bouquet* There's no rule to say that the bride must carry a bouquet, but most do, as flowers add a decorative touch and give the nervous bride something to do with her hands. Etiquette says that the bride should not carry flowers if she opts to wear a hat instead of a veil, but like many oldfashioned customs, this one is made to be broken! Traditionally, the bride throws her bouquet as she leaves the reception. Superstition says the catcher of the bouquet will be the next to marry.

*Boutonnieres* are usually worn by the bridegroom, best man, groomsmen, and fathers of the couple. Traditionally, they are worn on the left lapel. Make sure boutonnieres are securely fastened—a groomsman should carry pins in case of emergency.

*Corsages* may be worn by the mothers and grandmothers of the couple. Corsages are pinned on to the outfit, usually on the shoulder or lapel, or strapped to the wrist. With clothes made of fine fabric, the corsage should be light so it doesn't drag or tear.

*Confetti* Check with your wedding venue that they're happy for your guests to throw confetti. Paper confetti is available in many shapes and colors, but there are alternatives. Try dried or fresh flower petals, or bottles of soap bubbles for guests to blow at you.

# transportation

♡  The groom and best man normally travel to the ceremony under their own steam, while the bride is treated to something special that then takes the newlyweds to their reception.

♥  The bride and her father (or whoever is giving her away) travel together. The mother of the bride and the bridesmaids travel in the same car (or two, if they can't all fit in one). They leave for the ceremony before the bride and her father.

♡  Traveling to your wedding in a vintage car or horsedrawn carriage is far from essential, but it's one of the things that makes the day fun and special. Any car can be smartened up with a wash and polish, and the addition of ribbons or flowers. Alternatives to a carriage or vintage car include modern limousines and sports cars.

### Transportation tips

♥ Think about practicalities such as the time of year and the weather—important considerations if you want an open carriage—and your dress, which may take up a fair bit of room.

♡ Book as far ahead of your wedding as possible to be sure of getting what you want.

♥ Visit companies to check their vehicles are well maintained.

♡ Get a written estimate—check whether charges are by the hour or are at a set rate, and how much mileage is included. Ask whether your transport will be decorated, and if the chauffeur or coachman will be in uniform.

♥ If you're booking an old car, ask what happens if it breaks down. Will an alternative be available?

# the processional and recessional

♥ The bride does not have to be given away. She can walk down the aisle alone, if she wishes, or even be accompanied by her groom. As wedding traditions become increasingly open to reinterpretation, more and more brides ask mothers, siblings, or step-parents to give them away. At Jewish weddings, the bride is escorted by both parents—a tradition some non-Jewish brides are beginning to adopt.

♡ The bridegroom and best man wait at the top of the aisle. Groomsmen may stand at the top of the aisle or head the procession, walking in pairs. The bridesmaids follow them. The maid or matron of honor enters next. Alternatively, groomsmen and bridesmaids may enter together, walking in pairs, followed by the honor attendant and best man. Flower girls or ring bearers are last down the aisle before the bride, who walks down the aisle on the left arm of her father (or whoever is giving her away). The bride hands her bouquet to her maid of honor (or mother) during the service.

♥ After the ceremony the bride and groom walk back up the aisle. Any flower girls or ring bearers follow, then the honor attendant and the best man, then the bridesmaids and groomsmen, walking in pairs.

# The Reception

The reception offers a chance to celebrate after the solemnity of the ceremony and the marriage vows. There are few hard and fast rules about how things should be done, so it's up to you whether or not you observe tradition.

# reception timetable

♡ The bride and groom should arrive first at the reception, followed by the bridesmaids, best man, maid of honor, and both sets of parents.

♥ A traditional receiving line is a way of welcoming your guests personally. The usual order is: bride's mother and father, groom's mother and father, bride, groom, maid of honor, and best man. Bridesmaids and groomsmen are not included. If you don't want a formal receiving line, just you and your groom could welcome people. With lots of guests, a receiving line can be lengthy.

♡ The meal. This can be a sit-down meal or a buffet.

♥ The toasts (see page 56). Traditionally, these take place after the meal, but nowadays some couples choose to have them before, so the bride's father, the groom, and the best man can relax and enjoy their meal.

♡ The cutting of the cake (see page 60).

♥ Receptions often go on into the evening, with a dance after the toasts and cake, or after a short break.

♡ The departure of the bride and groom.

# the seating plan

♥ If you're having an informal buffet, you may want your guests to sit wherever they want. For a sit-down meal, a seating plan is a good idea, as it avoids a scramble for places.

♡ Your aim is to put together people who'll enjoy each other's company. Some guests will already know each other. Otherwise, bear in mind a few guidelines. People of the same age are usually best together. Look for things that guests have in common: their children, their jobs, and their interests.

♥ Try for a mixture of extroverts and those who need drawing out, and for a balance of men and women. Work single people into the plan early on so you don't use them as "fillers".

♡ Married couples should be on the same table, but not next to each other. It's considered polite to place close family and older friends on tables close to the top table.

♥ The bride and groom usually take their seats last so that everyone can applaud them as they come in. The top table is also normally served with food first.

| maid of honor | groom's father | bride's mother | groom | bride | bride's father | groom's mother | best man |
|---|---|---|---|---|---|---|---|

**Traditional top table seating plan**

The seating plan itself is usually displayed at the entrance to the reception. The plan can be a printed list or you may want to make it into a feature, having it handwritten or decorated in some way. Another approach is to write guests' names and table numbers on little cards, with or without envelopes, and place these on a table for people to collect as they enter.

*The top table* This is traditionally for the wedding party only, including the bride and groom, both sets of parents, the best man, and the maid of honor.

♡ If your and/or your fiancé's parents are divorced and remarried, you'll have to decide whether you want step-parents seated on the top table.

♥ If one parent has remarried but the other has not, it's an idea to find an escort for the unmarried one to balance the table. Perhaps a son or daughter or brother or sister could fill in.

♡ Remember that you and your fiancé's parents should be either side of you as on the traditional plan, with step-parents added on to either end, alternating between men and women.

| step-father | maid of honor | groom's father | bride's mother | groom | bride | bride's father | groom's mother | best man | step-mother |
|---|---|---|---|---|---|---|---|---|---|

*Alternative top table seating plan (with step-parents)*

# the toasts

♥ There can be few grooms, fathers, or best men who positively look forward to giving their toast. However, toasts are an important part of a wedding and provide an opportunity to voice the thoughts and emotions that the day gives rise to.

♡ The traditional order of toasts is as follows: the bride's father (or whoever gave her away); the groom; then the best man.

♥ Nowadays, more and more brides and/or maids of honor are opting to speak too. They can be slotted in wherever seems appropriate, but make sure all the toasts don't run on for too long—try to keep them to 30 minutes in total.

Delivering a speech is always nerve-racking. Here are ten steps to a flawless performance:

♥ Keep to the point—speak for five to ten minutes at most.

♡ Look up, smile, and look around at the guests. If you look happy and confident, you'll probably sound it, too.

♥ If you're not naturally witty, don't try too hard. Be sincere and speak from the heart.

♡ Prepare well in advance—not the night before.

♥ Practice your speech out loud a few times and time it to make sure it doesn't overrun. If possible, read it to someone whose opinion you trust.

♡ If you're an inexperienced speaker, write the speech out in full rather than in note form.

♥ Be funny if you can, but avoid sexual innuendoes or anything risqué. Elderly relatives will be listening as well as your friends, so it must be suitable for all.

♡ Keep your sentences short and your language conversational and informal.

♥ If you're not used to speaking in public, use a microphone if there is one. If not, lift your head and project your voice—don't mutter into your notes. You'll need to speak up to be heard at the back of the room.

♡ Don't rush, or you'll fall over your words. Take a deep breath and take your time.

## who speaks and what they should say

### The bride's father

His toast focuses on his daughter. He should say:

♥ How pleased he is to see so many family members and friends at the wedding.

♡ How proud he is of his daughter (he may want to recount some stories from her childhood).

♥ How happy he is to welcome his new son-in-law into the family.

♡ He finishes with a toast to "the bride and groom."

### The groom

He follows on from and answers the bride's father, thanking him for the toast (he usually manages to get in a mention of his "wife," which is guaranteed to prompt applause!). His main duty is thanking people:

♥ Everyone who's come to the wedding.

♡ Everyone who's helped to organize the wedding, such as both sets of parents (and anyone else who's contributed financially or otherwise).

♥ His parents for all their help and support over the years (here, he may give a gift or bouquet to his and the bride's mother).

♡ His best man.

♥ His wife for marrying him and being such a beautiful bride.

♡ The attendants for doing such a good job.

♥ He finishes by toasting "absent friends," then "the bridesmaids" (not forgetting the flower girls and ring bearers).

## The best man

He has a real challenge, as he is expected to be funny. His toast should be tasteful, inspirational, and short, avoiding anything smutty or embarrassing. In addition, he should:

♥ Thank the groom for his words and his toast to the attendants.
♡ Read out any messages or cards from absent friends.
♥ Recount some amusing anecdotes about the groom.
♡ Talk about the bride and say what a good couple she and the groom make.
♥ He finishes by toasting "Mr. and Mrs. ..." and announcing the cutting of the cake.

# the cake

The traditional order of events is for cake-cutting to follow the speeches, when everyone's eyes are on the couple. However, nowadays, catering staff often encourage couples to cut the cake before the speeches so that they can take it away and prepare it to be served with coffee afterwards.

♥ The classic wedding cake is a rich fruit mixture, made into three tiers (normally supported by little columns, though it's also popular now to have them stacked), and covered with marzipan and white royal icing.

♡ Fruit cake keeps well and couples often follow the custom of preserving the top tier for the christening of their first child. If you want to do this, remove the icing and marzipan, wrap the cake in waxed paper and store in a cool, dark place.

♥ It's a nice idea to send small pieces of cake to people who can't attend the wedding.

*Alternative ideas for wedding cake:*

♥ Chocolate, lemon, coffee, or carrot cake, or plain poundcake. Remember that if you want a frosted cake, the cake itself must be fairly firm so as not to collapse.

♡ French croquembouche, a spectacular pyramid of cream-filled choux-pastry buns topped with caramel or spun sugar. If you want one, find an expert to make it—croquembouche is difficult to make and has to be served very fresh.

♥ Ice-cream cake, pavlova, cheesecake, or, to follow one sweet-toothed bride's example, three huge banana and toffee pies on a tiered cake stand.

♡ A miniature wedding cake for each guest (most practical at small weddings) or individual sponge cakes served with a fruit coulis, crème Anglaise, or chocolate sauce in place of dessert.

♥ Individual cupcakes or tarts, topped with frosting, crystallized flowers, or berries.

*Decoration* The inspiration for your cake could come from any number of sources: you and your fiancé's shared interests; your wedding venue; the time of year; or the flowers and colors you are using. You could have a novelty cake, made to look like a pile of wedding presents, for instance, a giant heart or bow, or perhaps an open book of love poetry.

# resources

## Wedding websites

*www.awebwedding.com*
Links to wedding vendors in your local area as well as an online gift registry and a library full of useful wedding information.

*www.exclusivelyweddings.com*
Online store offering a huge selection of favors, gifts for attendants, decorations, cake tops, and many other wedding essentials.

*www.theknot.com*
Comprehensive general wedding website complete with user-friendly planning tools, vendor listings, practical information, and a wedding store.

*www.topweddingsites.com*
Wedding planning links and information

*www.ultimatewedding.com*
Lots of essential information as well as thousands of links to wedding websites offering a wide variety of wedding services.

*www.virtuallymarried.com*
Create your own wedding website, with fun polls and quizzes as well as lots of practical information for guests, including registry details, maps, and other useful information.

*www.weddingchannel.com*
Comprehensive source for wedding gowns, cakes, bouquets, and hairstyles.

Also offers an online wedding organizer and a gift registry for a large number of diverse stores.

*www.weddingfavorites.com*
Stylish favors for weddings and showers.

*www.weddingwebsites.com*
Create a personal online information resource for friends and family. Fun details are combined with useful information for guests.

*www.weddingzone.net*
Search for wedding services nationwide and browse the wedding superstore. Also links to other wedding sites.

# picture credits

Key a– above, b=below, l=left, r=right, c=center

### Polly Wreford
Pages 1, 6-7, 9-11, 22, 23, 28-29, 30-31, 33l, 33ar, 33acr, 34bl, 34br, 36, 39l all, 43br, 48a, 48br, 52l, 52cr, 52br, 56, 57, 60 background, 60 inset above, 62, 63, endpapers

### Caroline Arber
Pages 8, 12bc, 12br, 15ar, 15c, 15br, 18l, 18ar, 20b all, 24l all, 26, 27, 33bcr, 34a, 40b all, 43ar, 44, 45, 46, 47, 48bc, 50al, 50ar, 50b, 51, 64cr, 64r

### Dan Duchars
15l, 16a, 18cr, 18br, 20a, 33br, 37, 40a, 41, 43l, 50ac, 64cl

### Viv Yeo
Pages 12a, 12bl, 13, 21, 24r, 25, 59l, 59r, 64 l

### Craig Fordham
Pages 2-3, 5, 15bc, 16b, 17, 35, 39r

### David Brittain
Pages 4, 48bl, 49, 52ar, 55, 61,

### Peter Cassidy
Pages 32, 34bc, 58, 59c

### Sandra Lane
Page 60 inset below

# acknowledgments

*The publisher would like to thank everyone who made the photography for this book possible. Special thanks go to the brides and grooms: Annabel and David, Catherine and Scott, Lizzie and Justin, and Berenice and Jamie for so graciously allowing us to photograph their beautiful weddings. Thanks also to our beautiful little 'flower girls'—Arianna, Niamh, Rita, Shannon, and Stella.*